POSTCARDS from Paul

EPHESUS

CHRISTIAN FOCUS PUBLICATIONS

Illustrations by James P Smith
Written and designed by Hazel Scrimshire

Printed in Singapore

© 1994
Christian Focus Publications

Geanies House,

Fearn, Tain,

Ross-shire, IV20 1TW

SCOTLAND

Dear Reader,

You may be wondering who I am and why I have written so many postcards. My name is Paul and I was around quite a long time ago...

So many exciting things happened to me that I decided to write to my friends and tell them all about it. I used to hate the church and did all I could to destroy it, until one day, when I had an amazing experience.

It all started when I was on my way to a city called Damascus...I'll let you read the rest for yourself!

Paul.

PS: If you want to find out some more details, take a look in the Bible in the book of Acts.

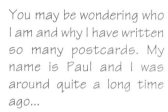

DAMASCUS

Dear Friends,

I must tell you about my adventure on the way to Damascus. I was going to that city to arrest followers of Jesus, when something amazing happened on the way.

My friends and I were nearing the city, when suddenly, we were stopped by a blinding light from heaven. It flashed around me and I fell to the ground with surprise. You can imagine how I felt when a voice spoke to me.

It was Jesus whom I heard! He told me to go into the city, and from there I would be shown what to do.

At first, my friends were so shocked they could not speak. They had heard the sound, but had not seen anyone. I felt very shaken too, but stood up and opened my eyes. Then I made a terrible discovery. Although my eyes had been opened to see Jesus, I found that I could no longer see.

With the help of my friends, we continued our journey to Damascus, where I had more incredible experiences . I'll write again later.

God be with you,

Paul.

DAMASCUS

Dear Friends,

We arrived in Damascus at last! It was frightening being blind! I was taken to a house on Straight Street, where a man called Ananias prayed with me. Imagine my amazement when suddenly I could see again! It was wonderful! I was baptised, and was later so excited that I went to the synagogues and started to preach the good news.

I must admit that some people were a little suspicious. They knew that I'd tried to destroy the Church and didn't trust me. Other people heard me preaching about Jesus and became so angry that they plotted to kill me!

It's a risky life being a follower of Jesus, but the Lord is a great protector. When they learned about the threat against my life, my new friends made an escape plan. They took me to the city walls at night, and I was lowered down to safety in a basket.

I am now in Jerusalem and will write soon with more news.

Paul.

Dear Friends,

I had some difficulties with the believers in Jerusalem. Many did not believe that I was a true follower of Jesus and were afraid. Thankfully, a man called Barnabas spoke up for me. He told the others about my journey on the Damascus road and the change in my life. They believed him, and I was invited to stay among them.

I spent some time talking about the Lord to the Jews in Jerusalem, but they reacted violently. After more attempts to kill me, it was felt that I should leave. The believers took me to Caesarea, and from there I was sent to Tarsus.

Although it has not been an easy time, I am delighted that the Church has grown.

I will let you know when another mission is planned.

Paul.

TARSUS

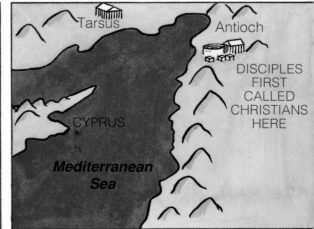

Tarsus

Antioch

CYPRUS

DISCIPLES
FIRST
CALLED
CHRISTIANS
HERE

*Mediterranean
Sea*

Dear Friends,

I must tell you about my friend Barnabas. He is a faithful servant of the Lord and has encouraged many people. We went to Antioch and spent some time with the believers there. I'm not sure how it's happened, but those who claim to be followers of Jesus, have been given the name 'Christian'.

I don't know whether you have heard of Agabus, the prophet. The Lord spoke through him and said that there would be a bad famine all over the country. The other disciples thought it would be good to help out the believers in Judea. Barnabas and I have been asked to take money to the church elders there.

I'll tell you more about our next journey later.

Yours in Christ,

Paul.

Dear Friends,

After finishing our last mission, we spent some time fasting and praying. We felt the Holy Spirit telling us to visit the island of Cyprus and another believer, called John Mark came along to help. We set off from Seleucia and landed on the island. What an experience!

We had been asked to preach by the Governor of the island. However, on reaching Paphos, we were interrupted by a magician who said that he was a prophet. He wanted to stop us preaching the good news about Jesus.

I knew that the man was up to no good and spoke strongly against him. The next moment he was struck blind.

The Governor who had been watching and listening was convinced by our message. We thank God that he too, became a believer!

It wasn't long before we were on the move again. This time we went to Perga. When I have time, I will write again soon.

God be with you,

Paul.

PERGE

PISIDIAN ANTIOCH

Pisidian Antioch

Perga

CYPRUS

Paphos

Dear Friends,

When we arrived at Perga, our friend John Mark decided to leave us and return to Jerusalem. We continued our journey, and moved on to Pisidian Antioch.

While we were at the synagogue I was invited to speak. It was good to share the news of Jesus, and I was pleased to be invited back the next week.

When we returned I couldn't believe how many people had come to hear us. It must have been nearly the whole city. However, this upset some Jews and they began to cause trouble. In spite of their reaction, many people became believers.

The situation in Antioch became so dangerous that we had to leave the area. We were glad to see that, although they were being treated badly, the followers were joyful.

I will keep you informed of my next journey.

Paul.

LYSTRA

Pisidian Antioch

Iconium

Derbe

Perga

Lystra

Dear Friends,

We had an exciting time at Iconium. At the synagogue, God greatly blessed us and many believed our message. Amazing miracles took place, but once again, some people deliberately caused trouble. We finally had to escape to Lystra because of a plot to stone us.

While preaching at Lystra, God used us to perform a miracle. I noticed a man among us who was disabled, and commanded him to get up. The next minute he was on his feet and jumping around.

After the miracle the crowd thought we were gods and wanted to bring us sacrifices. I tried to stop them, telling them it was God they should be worshipping. Then the mood changed and people started to throw stones at me. I became unconscious and was hauled out of the city.

Thankfully, some believers have helped me and I have been able to go back to the city. As you will see, life has not been easy.

I will be in touch again soon.

God be with you,

Paul.

LYSTRA

Dear Friends,

After our frightening experiences, life began to calm down. We decided to go from Derbe to some of the places we had visited before. It was good to see that although other believers had suffered too, their faith was strong.

It wasn't long before trouble started in Antioch. There was a long debate about certain laws in the scriptures. Then I had an upsetting argument with Barnabas, and we decided to go our separate ways. He set off for Cyprus with John Mark, and I went through Syria and Cilicia with Silas. We returned to Derbe and Lystra where a friend called Timothy joined us.

We stopped at Troas where I had a vision - it was like a dream. I could see a man, and he was pleading for us to come over to Macedonia to help him. We felt that this was an urgent mission and prepared to go straight away.

I will let you know what happened next when I have more time.

Paul.

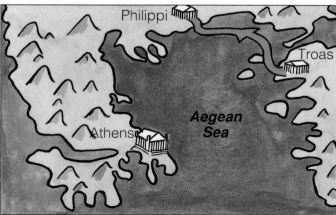

Dear Friends,

We sailed from Troas and travelled to several places. We stopped at Philippi for a few days and were excited by what happened there.

We had been looking for somewhere to pray and found a place outside the city. We sat beside a river where some women were gathered. After talking to them for some time, I noticed that one woman was very interested in what we were saying. She was a purple cloth dealer called Lydia. She accepted Jesus and was so overjoyed that she told her family. It was a privilege to baptise them all.

Lydia invited us to stay at her home, an offer we gratefully accepted. We have been facing more persecution since then. I'll give you more details as soon as I can.

Paul.

PHILIPPI

PHILIPPI

Dear Friends,

It is exciting to be a follower of Jesus! I must tell you about our next adventure.

We were in Philippi, and were being followed by a slave girl who could tell fortunes. She knew all about us and kept shouting abuse. I was disturbed by the girl, who needed to be set free from an evil spirit. Jesus enabled me to command the spirit from the girl, and she was very relieved.

The girl's owners were furious when they saw that she would not make money for them again, and brought us before the magistrates. They told lies about us and a whole crowd of people stirred up trouble. We were badly beaten and thrown into prison. However, God allowed good to come from all the pain. I will tell later how it all happened.

God be with you,

Paul.

Dear Friends,

Last time I told you about our struggles. However, the Lord is always with us. After Silas and I were put in prison we began to pray and praise God. As we sang, the other prisoners began to listen. Suddenly, there was a massive earthquake. All the doors flew open, the ground shook and our chains fell off. We were free!

In the chaos, I noticed that the prison warden was about to commit suicide. He thought that we had all escaped, and was very afraid. I told him to put away his sword and assured him that we were all still there. The warden was so relieved and surprised that he asked how he could become a believer. He and his whole family accepted Jesus, and we were filled with joy. Later, he took us to his house and gave us a meal.

The next day the local authorities released us. What a turn around! We have certainly had an eventful time.

Paul.

Dear Friends,

Life is never dull while on a mission for God.

We went to Thessalonica and as usual, I went to the synagogue to preach. However, some jealous trouble makers stirred up a riot. They became even angrier when they couldn't find us. We managed to escape when it was dark and slipped off to Berea.

Once again I began to preach and was attacked, so we had to move to another place. My companions, Silas and Timothy stayed behind and I went on ahead to Athens.

I felt very upset because the city is full of idols. It made me determined to speak out about Jesus. I challenged some philosophers there, and although some people laughed, others listened carefully and accepted the message.

I am on my way to Corinth and will write again soon.

Paul.

ATHENAE

Dear Friends,

I have met an interesting couple called Priscilla and Aquila who are tentmakers, like me. I worked with them for a while but on the sabbath spoke in the synagogue. Some people made threats against me and would not accept what I was saying.

Silas and Timothy joined me in Corinth and I spent most of my time preaching. I was encouraged when Crispus, (the synagogue ruler) and his whole family became believers.

The Lord spoke to me through a vision. He told me not to be frightened by all the persecution I have faced and has promised to protect me. I will be staying here for some time but will keep in touch.

Paul.

CORINTHUS

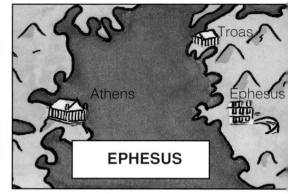

EPHESUS

Dear Friends,

My travels took me to Ephesus recently. I met up with some Christians and asked them if they had received the Holy Spirit. They seemed puzzled by the question. I prayed with them and baptised them in the name of Jesus. The Holy Spirit touched their lives and they began to speak in new languages, just as the disciples did on the day of Pentecost. It was an exciting time.

Many people in Ephesus who had followed false teaching, burned their occult books. However, those who made the idols were very angry because people would not buy their goods any more. They stirred the crowds into a real frenzy, and there was another riot. The disciples wouldn't let me try to calm them down.

Thankfully, the governor in charge of the town managed to quieten them down (much to my relief). I will be in contact with you soon.

Paul.

TROAS

Dear Friends,

After surviving yet another dangerous situation, I set off for Macedonia. I travelled around that area and then spent some time with friends at Troas. On the Saturday night we gathered together for a meal and talked for a while. While I was speaking, someone suddenly dropped dead! Not from my preaching, but from tiredness. He had fallen from the third floor and died straight away.

I went over to the young man and took hold of him, telling the others not to be alarmed and that he was alive. Then we returned to our meeting. Praise God, the man who had fallen was able to return home - to the amazement of the others.

When it was time for me to leave, I was upset at the thought of not seeing them again. However, I have not had time to stay sad as I am preparing for another journey. I will write soon when I arrive at my next destination.

Paul.

JERUSALEM

Miletus
Patara

CYPRUS

Tyre

Ptolemais
Caesarea
Jerusalem

Dear Friends,

Since leaving you, I have visited many places. In Caesarea I had some disturbing news. A prophet there told me that if I went to Jerusalem, my life would be in danger. However, I was not put off.

I arrived in Jerusalem, and found that the Christians there were confused by some of my teaching. I tried to clear up the problem, but was disturbed by the reaction of some Jews. They thought I was spreading a false message and dragged me out of the temple. I knew that they were trying to kill me, and was relieved when some soldiers came to break up the riot.

The soldiers handcuffed me, and when I asked if I could try and calm the crowd they became really angry. They were going to beat me, until I told them that I was a Roman. As you know, it is against the law to beat a Roman. Once again the Lord protected me.

I will write soon and let you know how I was set free.

God be with you,

Paul.

Dear Friends,

Those who were in charge of the city wanted to know why the Jews disliked me. I was brought before a group from the council, but as I spoke, they argued among themselves. I had to be removed from the scene, in case I was attacked. I was later told that there was a vicious plot to murder me - yet again! For my own safety, I was secretly moved to Caesarea by night. The soldiers guarded me until it was time for my trial.

I was brought before a group of important men, and a governor called Felix led the trial. They weren't able to bring any charges against me, and I was sent back to my cell.

I didn't realise that this case would go on for so long. However, in spite of the problems I faced being cooped up in prison, I was able to tell the people there about Jesus.

I will be in touch as soon as I can.

Yours in Christ,

Paul.

Dear Friends,

I can't believe I have been here for two years. Since last writing, there have been some changes. A man named Festus has taken charge of my case.

When questioned, I defended myself without a lawyer. It was exhausting! At the end of my defence I claimed my right to appeal to Caesar. I don't think they knew how to cope with me, but they agreed to my request.

Before leaving, a king called Agrippa arrived and a big fuss was made of him. I had to appear before him, and took the opportunity to share the gospel. I told him about meeting Jesus on the Damascus road, and how much he had changed me. Festus interrupted, shouting that too much studying had gone to my head. I had to assure him that I was not mad.

At last it was decided that I wasn't guilty of any crime. I would have been set free if I had not said earlier that I had wanted to see the Emperor in Rome. This has been the start of yet another adventure.

Peace be with you,

Paul.

CAESAREA

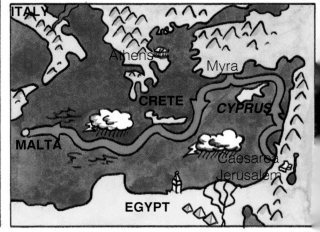

ITALY

Athens

Myra

CRETE

CYPRUS

MALTA

Caesarea

Jerusalem

EGYPT

Dear Friends,

The journey to Rome was awful! The sea was very choppy and made sailing dangerous. We stopped several times on the way, but had to go slowly because of high winds. I tried to convince the sailors that we should stay in the nearest harbour, but they wouldn't listen to me. We carried on to Crete, and the weather became much worse.

During a terrible storm, an angel appeared on the ship. He told me that we would all be kept alive. I told the others the good news, but don't think they were convinced.

We ended up throwing everything off the ship and heading for land.

The ship hit the sand and we were forced to jump overboard. God kept his promise though, and everyone reached the shore alive.

Since landing we have had a strange experience and I will give more details in time.

God be with you.

Paul.

MELITA

ROME

SICILY

Rome

Syracuse

MALTA

Dear Friends,

After the shipwreck, we found that we'd been washed up on an island called Malta. The local people were very kind to us and made a fire.

I had a fright when a snake escaped from the heat and clung onto my hand! I shook it off, relieved that it had not bitten me. However, after seeing that I had not died or become ill, the people thought I was a god. The Lord enabled me to heal many on the island, and we were honoured by the people.

When the weather calmed down we set off again and after stopping a few times we arrived at Rome.

I was delighted to be met by many believers, and grateful that at least I had a place of my own (although I was still being guarded). I was given the chance to share the good news with many Jews who hadn't heard about the fuss in Jerusalem. However, it was not long before they began to argue as well.

I must admit that after all my adventures and much travelling, it is good to stay in one place for a while. It has been great to write to you, and wonderful to share the good news which I hope you too have received.

Paul.

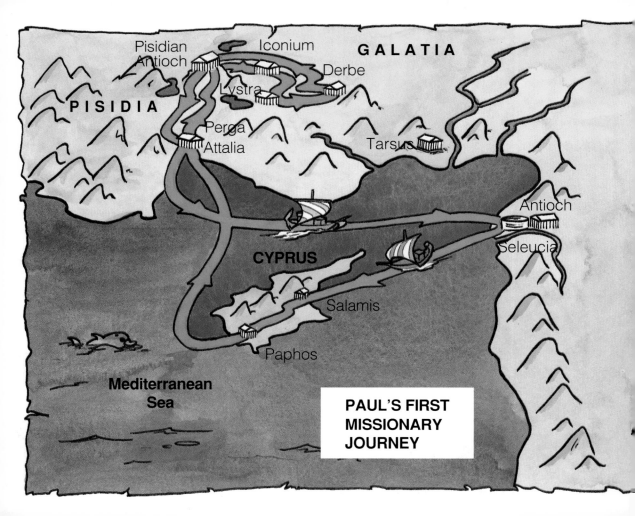

Pisidian Antioch · Iconium · GALATIA · Derbe · Lystra · PISIDIA · Perga · Attalia · Tarsus · Antioch · Seleucia · CYPRUS · Salamis · Paphos · Mediterranean Sea

PAUL'S FIRST MISSIONARY JOURNEY

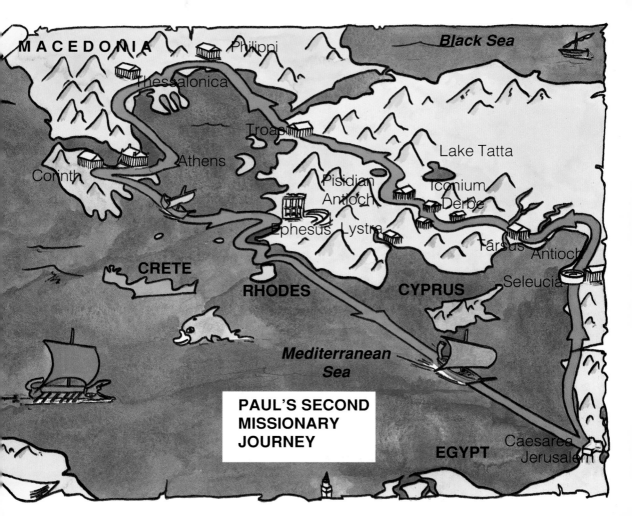

PAUL'S SECOND MISSIONARY JOURNEY

PAUL'S THIRD
MISSIONARY
JOURNEY

Another exciting event took place while Paul was on Malta.
Can you write and tell his friends what happened? - P.T.O.

MALTA

PS: If you need some help, turn to the Bible and look up the book of Acts, chapter 28: 1-10.

Dear Friends,